FOOD FOR THOUGHT
JERMAINE L. STEARNS

Copyright: 2018
All Rights Reserved
Printed in the United States of America
ISBN: 978-0-692-10396-8

Dedication

This cookbook is dedicated to all the influential individuals
who have shaped my world of cooking.

In loving memory of

Lonnell W.J. Stearns

To my father, Benjamin Stearns Jr.

To my wife, Roni D. Stearns and our children, Jerni Lonnell, Jordan Lily, and Josiah Levi Stearns. The Stearns & Wilson Familly,

Bishop Wayman J. Kirkman Sr.
Teresa Bazel-Wilson & Family, Ruby Floyd, Tara Melvin, Charlese Gibbs,
Marcus & Mikki Alexander & and to V.C.D.C Ministries for your love and support!

Lonnell W. J. Stearns
1953-2007

Table Of Contents

EARLY MORNING.................................PG. 7
FALLING CAKE...................................PG. 10
LEFTOVERS......................................PG. 14
                                                PG. 25
REFLECTION.....................................PG. 38
A MIRACLE TO SERVE........................PG. 42
SWEET WORDS................................PG. 51
LIFE NUGGET...................................PG. 54
SERVICE WITH A SMILE.....................PG. 58
                                                PG. 62
WHICH WAY SHOULD I GO?...............PG. 76
UNTIL FOREVER................................PG. 89
J. STEARNS......................................PG. 92

Introduction

Food For Thought is a book comprised of stories, recipes, and inspirational nuggets that I believe will empower your mind, body and soul. It is my goal that when you read this book, you will walk away with thought-provoking statements and questions that will help you become a better you. Food is meant to leave you full and fulfilled because it is hearty to the body and spirit. It is my prayer that the recipes and life experiences I share with you will allow you to walk away feeling the love and passion that God, family, and food can have in your life. I'm not writing to be famous, but I'm writing to share my story! Happy reading and cooking!

Early Morning

Waking up to the smell of food was always a joy in the morning in the Stearns's House. I distinctly remember the sound of wrestling pots and pans mixed with the sweet aroma of bacon floating throughout the house. Breakfast was the highlight of the morning! Since breakfast is the most important meal of the day, it was rarely, if ever missed in our house. If it wasn't my father cooking, it was my mother and later it became me. As a young boy, sitting at the table waiting to be served in order to take on the challenge of grits with butter, salt and pepper, just did something for me. They were warm and inviting and made me feel comfortable. What's a full breakfast without grits? I occasionally added cheese to mine, but my brother took his grits to another level. He would take all of the other sides, like the eggs, bacon or sausage, and mix them together in the grits and then he would add ketchup, which made it look horrible! Either way, I did experience the concoction, and to my surprise, it was not half bad. The simple way has always been my way.

Smells have a power trait to them, they can bring back a memory and evoke your emotions. As you prepare these recipes for breakfast I encourage you to speak to God and allow him to be the first experience of your day. Allow him to feed you your first meal as you prepare to feed others theirs. Take a moment to break the bread of life, which is the word of God and then add a drink of prayer and song. Get your system ready to receive to pour out.

Breakfast is full of substance and can take you a long way throughout your day. Eat the Word and allow it to minister to you.

Breakfast Salad

1 green, yellow, orange & red bell pepper
1 sweet or yellow onion
1-2 portabella mushrooms
2 cups of fresh spinach
2 to 4 boiled eggs
2 slices of pork or turkey bacon

Directions

Boil and peel eggs. Cook bacon until crispy. Chop all vegetables to your desire.

In frying pan, add enough EVOO (Extra Virgin Olive Oil) to coat the bottom of the pan. Sauté vegetables in layers. 1. Onions, until tender and then add peppers. Allow to simmer for about 4 minutes and then finally place the mushrooms, marrying all the vegetables together. Season to taste with house season (salt, pepper, parsley, and basil).

Plating

Layer the bottom of your plate with spinach (as much as you desire). Place mixed vegetables on top, adding your crispy crumbled bacon next. Finally take your peeled boiled eggs(cut in half) and place on top as garnish.

Falling Cake

"Don't stomp I have a cake in the oven!" Ever heard that saying or something similar to that before? I would often hear that very phrase coming through the house on a Saturday evening or early Sunday morning. Momma would be in the kitchen baking a cake and she said it because she didn't want her cake to fall. Now, when I was younger and heard that saying, I literally thought that the cake would fall to the floor, but Momma didn't want her cake to crumble. You see crumbled cake isn't good for anyone due to the fact that it isn't completely whole and it's still raw in certain places.

In life there are going to be people and circumstances that would try to stomp on you and cause you to crumble and fall. We must guard ourselves from being damaged while we are still in the process of becoming whole! Baking a cake takes the right amount of time in the heat (oven) and if taken out to soon or introduced to harsh, vibrating movements, something could mess up when it is supposed to be beneficial to others.

It's ok to be in the heat, just as long you are in it for the entire duration and with someone in your life who would help guard your process so you will not fall. You see, we need people like that, the ones who know what it took to get to this process and the ones who know how to protect what's on the inside. In other words, a baker-- one who assists with the development process. Search your circle and hold tight to your bakers, for they may be the very ones to assist you from crumbling and falling!

Morning Pancakes

1 box of "Complete" pancake & waffle mix (Just add Water)

Vanilla extract

Ground cinnamon

Nutmeg

Butter

Directions

In a bowl, prepare pancake mix (follow instructions on box for the amount you desire to prepare). Add 2 Tbsp. of Vanilla extract, 2 tsp of nutmeg, and 1 to 2 Tbsp. of cinnamon to mixture and 2 Tbsp. of Butter melted and blend together.

Cook until bubbles begin to form on the top then flip. Serve as desired.

Suggested Toppings

Strawberries caramelized with butter and brown sugar

Bananas with powdered sugar

Breakfast Sandwich

1 egg
2 slices of French bread
Butter
Spinach
1 slice of American cheese
2 slices of tomatoes
Grilled onions
3 slices of mesquite turkey sandwich meat Mayo
Dijon mustard

Seasonings

Basil
Salt
Pepper

Directions

Sautee onions in a pan with 1Tbsp of butter and season to taste with pepper, salt. After onions have caramelized removed from pan and add 1Tbsp of EVOO to the pan. Fry egg to your liking. You may also want to warm your turkey in the same pan.

Butter your French bread slices and grill on a skillet until golden brown. After grilling the bread, spread mayo and mustard, after which add cheese, egg and top with turkey slices. Adding fresh spinach and tomato slices. Season with basil seasoning. Close sandwich.

"God doesn't become Lord in your life until you find yourself in a crisis!"

-Jermaine L. Stearns

Leftovers

The true meaning of lunch is a meal eaten in the middle of the day, typically one that is lighter or less formal than an evening meal. I never knew how important lunch was to me until I became a husband with a real job. When you enjoy eating you don't mind eating three meals a day. In fact, research shows that lunch is usually between 12:00 PM and 1:30 PM and is known as the snack time. Who doesn't like a snack? Do you know when the biggest lunch often takes place in the year? During the holidays; Christmas, Thanksgiving and even on Sundays. These are the at-home luncheons of any and all lunches.

For most of us, Sundays are filled with worship, family, and food. Sometimes before, after, or even during worship, we are already looking forward to eating. And the big question of the day is not necessarily what time does church start, but what are we eating after church? Lunch on these days were the most important meals we would have in our home. In fact, Sunday "dinner" which was really lunch, would be cooked on Saturday evenings. My God, how we would suffer in the house, smelling that food all night long and not being able to touch it. This type of lunch brought everyone from everywhere just to get a taste. It was merely impossible for you to stop by just to speak. Sooner or later you'd end up with a fork in your mouth and or a plate in your hand, wrapped in aluminum foil, toted in a grocery bag. It was this lunch that helped sooth, lift, and bring the family together.

Lunch usually consists of salad, soup, a light sandwich, and fruit. In my house, lunch is what is left over from dinner, especially Sundays . Some people don't eat leftovers, but I have come to find that leftovers are often better than the meal eaten the first time.

The word of God speaks of a remnant, where God is looking for a small quantity (leftovers) of individuals that would serve him after the storm (Romans 11:5) Will you be the leftovers?

Soulful Ingredient : As you go throughout your day and get ready for your lunch break, take a moment to dine with Christ . A light spiritual consumption can hold you until your evening intimate time with the savior. Reading a scripture or pondering over a sermon from Sunday worship has just the right amount of substance(leftover) to keep you. As you "feed your face", feed your soul, because a little luncheon goes a long way. Be the remnant to eat the leftovers. Somebody shout " I'll take the leftovers!"

Potato Soup

10 White potatoes (8 cups cubed)
Parsley
Green onions
1/2 Sweet onion
1 Garlic Clove (minced)
Butter (4 Tbsp & 2 Tbsp)
32 1/2 oz of chicken stock
Salt
Pepper
Milk
1/4 Cup Flour

Directions
Melt 4 Tbsp of butter in pot and add 1/2 sweet onion diced to the butter. Sautee until the onions are tender. Next, add the potatoes, cook until tender, stirring frequently. Once the potatoes are almost tender, add the garlic, salt, and pepper (season to taste). Upon mixing add the chicken stock, covering the potatoes. Bring potatoes with chicken stock to boil.

Once potatoes are fork tender, take out a 1 1/2 cup of potatoes and mash in a separate bowl. Once mashed add back to the simmering potatoes.

Cream
In a separate sauce pot, you will need to melt 2 Tbsp of butter and adding 1/4 flour. The butter and flour will make a paste. Next add your cup of milk and whisked until creamy. Then adding the cream to the soup (sample here to see if you need to add more salt). Allow to simmer for another 5 minutes, gently stirring.

Once completed, serve a bowl of soup, adding cheese, a few chopped green onions, a sprinkle of parsley. Served with butter grilled French bread.

Potato Soup

Grandpa's Soup

Inspired by Urius Fulwood, Jr.

1 tablespoon EVOO

1/2 stick of butter

1/2 large onion, chopped

2 cloves garlic, minced (optional)

1/3 cup ribs celery, chopped

1 cup carrots, sliced

1 cup green beans

1 cup fresh corn tidbits

1 cup potatoes diced

1/2 teaspoon salt

1 teaspoon oregano

2 to 3 containers of vegetable broth

Directions

Heat oil in a large soup or stock pot. Add EVOO & butter and the chopped onion, minced garlic, the carrots, and the celery. Heat, stirring, for 3-4 minutes, until onions are soft. Add the rest of the vegetables and heat for just another minute or two.

Add all seasoning to vegetables and adjust seasoning to taste. Once completed take vegetable stock and cover vegetables completely!

Allow to simmer on low until all vegetables are tender. Upon serving squeeze fresh lemon into each bowl and add parsley. Freshly grilled French Bread goes well with this recipe.

Urius Fulwood, Jr. (gone but never forgotten) & his granddaughter, Roni D. Fulwood Stearns.

Grandpa's famous soup, grown out of his own garden.
*The recipe in this book is not a replica of the recipe shown above.

Lonnell's Pasta Salad

1 2.25 oz can black olives

1 box grape tomatoes (sliced in 1/2)

1 pack turkey pepperoni

1 16oz box bowtie pasta

1/2 cup banana peppers

1 bottle zesty Italian dressing

1 bottle balsamic vinaigrette dressing

1/2 cheddar cheese

1/2 parmesan cheese

3 to 4 cucumbers (peeled and diced)

Directions

Place box of pasta in a pot of boiling water with a pinch of salt. Cook until pasta is tender, drain, and allow to cool.

Once pasta has cooled, add 1/2 tomatoes, 1/2 cup of cubed cheese, diced cucumbers, 1 can of black olives, turkey pepperoni, 1/2 cup of banana peppers. Then, add the bottles of dressings to mix. Add the 1/2 cup of mozzarella cheese, stir and allow to cool in refrigerator 30 minutes to 1 hour before serving.

Pasta Salad

"Don't give the enemy a platform!"
-Jermaine L. Stearns

Nettie's Eggrolls

1-2 bags finely shredded cabbage

1 small bag shredded carrots

1lb of ground turkey

1 8oz packaged mushrooms (dice very well)

1 package wonton wraps

1 to 2 bottles of Asian sweet & sour sauce

I cup of water

EVOO

Canola or vegetable oil

Directions

Begin by cooking the ground turkey in a pan until brown, season the turkey to taste with salt, pepper, garlic powder. After cooked, transfer to a dish and allow to sit. In the same pan add about 2 Tbsp of EVOO and 1 Tbsp of butter then place your shredded cabbage and carrots to the mix. Cook the two ingredients until tender, season with salt. After vegetables are prepared add the ground turkey back to the pan and mix together until nicely blended. After blending remove and allow to cool down.

In a deep fryer allow canola or vegetable oil to heat as you prepare the rolls. On a hard surface or cutting board, take one of the egg roll wraps and place about 3/4 of the mixture (ground turkey & vegetables) into the center. Take one end of the wrap and pull over the mixture, then dab water on the left and right corners and pull to the center allowing them to stick to the first end over mixture. Then dab water to the last corner and pull over, making a burrito out of the egg rolls.

Fry your rolls in the deep fryer and cook until golden brown (Be careful they will cook fast and could burn.)

Once cooked, serve hot and dip into the sweet and sour sauce. Enjoy!

"Never let anyone overtake you with their inadequacies. Their seed may birth an uproar of unpleasant characteristics that may be challenging to get rid of."

-Jermaine L. Stearns

Nettie's Egg Rolls

Something About Salad

1 to 2 lbs. of raw shrimp

1 box of pasta

2 turkey sausage links chopped

1 Tbsp. parsley

2/3 cup cilantro

1 Tbsp. crushed red peppers

1 pint heavy cream

1/2 stick of butter

Directions

In a large skillet, sauté shrimp in butter and olive oil mix and season with salt, pepper. Cook for about 8 minutes altogether turning on both sides. Once complete, remove shrimp and sauté your chopped sausage to the remnants of the shrimp

Cook your noodles in a large pot of water and season with 1tbsp of salt and 1tbsp of olive oil. Remove once tender and drain water off noodles.

Creamy Sauce

In a sauce pan, melt half of a stick of butter and add 1 pt. of heavy cream. Wisk together until cream thickens.

Once pasta, shrimp, and cream are all completed, marry them together in large skillet, adding 1Tbsp of parsley, 2/3 cup of cilantro and 1Tbsp of crush red peppers. Simmer for 5 minutes and serve hot or cold.

Something About Salad

"Stop trying to fit into circles that don't want you in them. It just will not work!"
-Jermaine L. Stearns

Spiritual Taste Buds

One of the major senses we possess as human beings is taste. The cluster of nerve endings that fill our mouth can fill our body with excitement when they encounter something good or can evoke a discomfort, depending on the ingredients. There are certain areas in our mouth that provide distinct tastes. They are known as sweet, salty, sour, and bitter. When we encounter these, they send signals to our brain to signify what we have experienced. These areas provide a wide range of emotions when utilized at certain times. These encounters leave an impression on us that we remember when we come in contact with that taste again; we can decide if it was good or bad for us.

We can learn a lot from our sense of taste and its flavors. One reason is that we must learn what is sweet, salty, sour, and bitter in our lives. You see, in order for us to know, we must experience the taste of what we like and don't like. Taste serves in so many ways that it would behoove us to take heed of the senses that we have, especially when it comes down to our relationship with God. The word of God says, "oh taste and see that the Lord is good!" We must have this experience in order to know.

There are so many different tastings that have been designed for us to enjoy eclectic foods, but if one is closed-minded they would never get the opportunity to enjoy some of the most amazing foods on the earth. Christ has provided us a buffet of opportunity to experience him. The sense that we have inside of us should provoke us to at least try and see that he is good. As you go throughout this book experience the different recipes and even tasting them. Remember to try Jesus first to get the first and true experience of real, authentic substance that you would enjoy telling everyone.

Crab Boil

In order for your seafood to taste great you need great seasoning! Here is my way of making your seafood taste great!

2 TBSP Salt

1 Whole onion

1 TBSP Pepper

2 garlic cloves

1/2 tsp Morton Nature's Seasoning

Directions

Boil a pot of water. Pour all of your ingredients into boiling water and place all of your desired seafood in the seasoning. Enjoy!

Salmon Patties

1 to 2 cans of Pink Salmon

½ Red bell pepper chopped

½ Onion chopped

½ cup of Breadcrumbs (homemade)

1 tsp Flour

½ tsp Salt

½ tsp Pepper

½ tsp Paprika

½ tsp Oregano

1 egg

Directions

Mix all ingredients together by hand in a mixing bowl! Once mixed well, create patties the size of the palm of your hand.

In a greased frying pan, place the palm sized patties no more than 3 to 4 at a time and allow them to cook until golden brown on both sides.

Once cooked, pair with a hot bowl of grits and bacon or basil rice and steamed veggies.

*precooked salmon works great!

Grilled Veggie Pack

Bell Peppers (All Colors) Onions

Mushrooms

2 Tbsp Butter

1 Tbsp Salt

1/2 tsp Pepper

1/2 tsp Italian Season

1/2 tsp Oregano

Directions

Cut all veggies to your desire sized. Once cut, place them in aluminum foil with butter and seasoning. Fold the foil over veggies and place on hot grill.

Allow veggies to cook until tender, the longer they sit the better they become.

Ben's Ribs

1 slab of pork ribs Salt
Pepper
Crush red peppers
Lawyer's seasoning
Brown sugar

Paprika

Base For Grilling

Water
Vinegar
Pepper

Directions

To ensure great ribs, make sure your grill is hot and ready! Rub your ribs down with an even amount of the seasoning and brown sugar on both sides, allow to sit for 4 hours in the refrigerator. Place on grill and cook on both sides until ribs are cooked all the way thru! Once completed allow ribs to sit for about 5 minutes before cutting!

Home Fries

5-8 Red or White Potatoes

Salt

Paprika

Vegetable oil

Sour cream

Directions

Cut potatoes into circles leaving the skin on. Rinse thoroughly! Allow potatoes to dry from rinse before frying them into hot grease. Once fries are slightly golden, take them out and while hot, season to taste with seasonings, and serve with sour cream on side!

Popping Pizza

"Eat right, live right, live right, do right!"
-Jermaine L. Stearns

Popping Pizza

1 pack of Boboli pizza crust

1 pack of ground turkey

1 pack of turkey pepperoni

1/2 half onion

1/2 cup of fresh chopped spinach

1 jar of marinara pizza sauce

1 Tbsp Oregano

1 Tbsp Italian Seasoning

Salt

Pepper

2 cloves chopped garlic

1/2 cup chopped mushroom

Directions

Pre heat oven to 350 degrees.

Cook ground turkey until completely done, seasoning with salt, pepper, and chopped garlic. Remove from pan and place in dish. Place all chopped vegetables in same pan and sauté, adding oregano, Italian seasoning. Cook vegetables until tender.

Mix ground turkey and vegetables together. Take your pizza crust and smear pizza sauce as first layer. Once completed, take your mixture and spread evenly on pizza crust. Next, add your fresh spinach on top as your third layer, then add your pepperoni as 4th layer. Finally, take your cheeses and cover entire pizza as your 5th layer.

Place in preheated oven, and cook until crust is golden brown and cheese has melted completely. Allow pizza to sit for 3 to 5 minutes before serving!

Spicy Grilled Corn

Fresh Corn on the Cob (in husk) Salt

Pepper

Butter

Sugar

Cayenne pepper

Directions

Mix all the seasonings together.

Take your fresh corn still (in husk) and allow to soak in water for 10-15 prior to grilling. Take the soaked corn and place on your grill (remember KEEP the husk on the corn). Allow to sit for about 25 minutes, turning the corn occasionally.

Once your corn is complete, pull the husk off! Coat corn in butter, and then season it with mix seasoning and serve. Your corn should be crispy and flavorful.

Chicken Noodle Soup

2 cups of chopped grilled chicken (one day old)

1/2 cup of Carrots

1 cup of Celery

3 bouillon cubes

1 box of vegetable stock

2 whole garlic cloves cut into halves

1/2 cup of chopped onion

1/2 cup of frozen or fresh corn

Parsley

Basil

Salt

Pepper

Directions

Combine all vegetable's, garlic and sauté in pot until tender. Once vegetable's have soften a little, add your chicken and cook just so chicken can marry with vegetable's. After which, add your seasoning and herbs and cover with vegetable stock and 3 bouillon cubes.

Allow soup to sit on stove for about 15 minutes and serve hot!

Go Green Greens

1 bunch of Collard Greens

1 Tbsp Salt

1/2 Tbsp Pepper

1 Tbsp Vinegar

1 Tbsp Parsley

2 slices of bacon

1 to 2 tsp of crush red peppers Sugar to taste

Directions

In a pot, fry your two slices of bacon until crispy. Once done, remove bacon and add pepper and parsley to grease. Take your chopped greens and add to the pot. Stir the greens once placed in the pot and cover.

Once greens have become tender and have darkened a little, add your sugar and crushed red peppers. Stir, next add one cup of water to the bottom. Allow greens to cook until done!

Reflection

Times in the kitchen with my family leave memories that even writing them down can't explain, but they were simply amazing times. As a child, we were not allowed in the kitchen often because "grown folks" were talking or working, but when the time was right, I saw and learned as much as I possible could. One of those moments was always around the time of the 4th of July. As a little boy I could hear the planning of who was going to purchase the hog and the stuff (ingredients for the hash). It usually came down to my grandparents and my parents going half on a whole hog to cook for dinner. We would go to the Piggly Wiggly and purchase a whole pig, case of chicken, bell peppers, onions, vinegar and so much more. When you're little everything had purpose to it and during the fourth, the purpose was to bring the family together and eat! Family from the neighborhood, and those who lived a few minutes way, somehow seemed to make their way just to see the hog and sample that good stuff (Hash and Rice).

We would sit at my grandparents' table that was too big for the kitchen but too small for everything to fit on it. The TV would be going, cigarette smoke would be in the air and drinks would be upon the table, The most important thing was that we were together making it happen. Yep, I was right in the midst. During "hash time", I would love to assist with the grinding of the meat. One year my grandfather had the grinder you had to turn the handle to make work, but it was short lived. I would take, liver, kidney, onions, bell peppers (all colors), and the head of the hog and grind it all in that machine and someone would mix it and throw it all into the pot on the stove. The smell wasn't too bad, neither was the taste, Let's just say it wasn't for me though. After it simmered for hours, my grandmother would make what we called "cha cha", the sauce that to go over the hash and rice. My, what a memory!

Somehow cooking just made things feel right. Even when there was something wrong or time had elapsed between fellowship, it was cooking that brought the family in the same area and things just flowed. And it wasn't one-sided either. The men and the women were cooking together inside the house, but the woman left the grilling up to my dad, even my granddaddy. Uncle Ben, as my late cousin, Ricky, called him, was the main griller. I have watched my father grill almost every weekend since I could remember. This was one of his many talents, cooking and mastering the grill. That hog would meet that grill the day before the 4th. He would get thawed, washed, and seasoned. My father would have an "outhouse stove" that would hold hot wood and charcoal to be added to the fire under the hog. This process was from sun up to sun down and back up again. Music would be playing and the laughter would always keep the party going with the assistance of the spirits, lol, hey, but it was what they did. I mean into the hours of the morning, the grill never stopped until he was finish. All night, the backyard would be jumping. I don't even think my dad got much sleep, in fact there was one moment, I can recall that my father had dozed off in the backyard. So sleep, no, but naps, yes! He managed to get the work done.

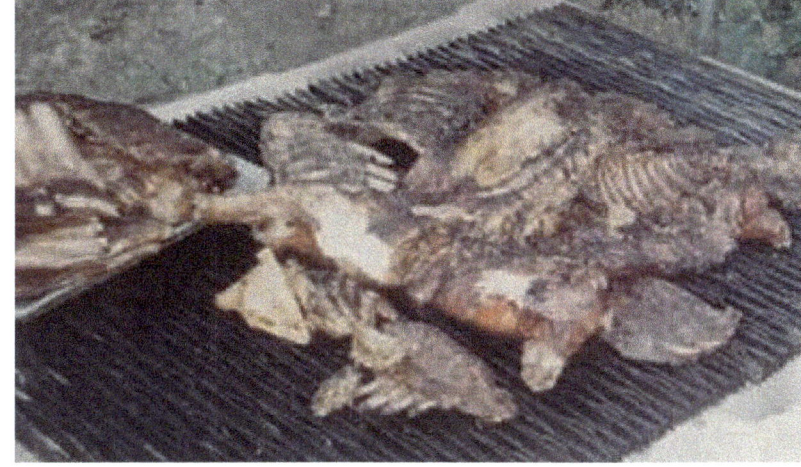

It's moment like these that families hardly possess anymore. One thing I have come to realize is that the joy and talent of cooking is good, but it's the love of family and wanting to feed the spirit of a person with love and laughter that makes the food and cooking process even better. Take a moment to ask yourself, when was the last time I cooked and fed someone with love and laughter? You see, it's not always about what you cook, but how much love you put into cooking that makes the difference. Cooking isn't just about putting something in a pot or in a dish, but it's about the purpose and the time spent in the process that makes the meal great. Take a second and think on your fondest memory of being in the kitchen preparing for someone or even being cooked for, that made you smile. Marinate on that thought when you start your next dish and I promise your efforts would not go unnoticed in preparing or receiving. Cook to feed but love to satisfy!

My Father, Ben aka Peewee, doing what he does best!

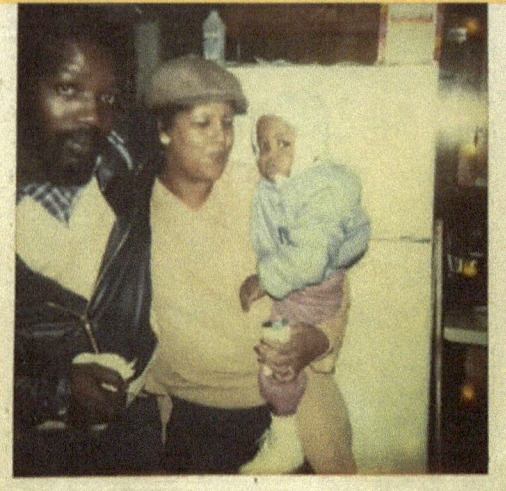

"False expectations of others can leave you damaged! Never expect something beyond their capabilities! STOP expecting orange juice to come from a lemon. It's just not going to work!"

-Jermaine L. Stearns

A Miracle To Serve

One of the greatest miracles in the Bible was Jesus turning water into wine, John 2:1-11. In fact, it was one of the first miracles he performed during a time of celebration and love. Isn't it amazing that even in performing the miracle at the wedding Jesus was still serving? Often times we go throughout our day looking for miracles signs and wonders, not knowing that serving others is a miracle within itself. Miracles are not only supernatural occurrences that happen during prayer time, or "church service", but they take place before our very eyes when one reaches to help someone else. It takes a person of humility, dedication, commitment, and selfless acts to serve others in this time and age. Most of us don't mind serving, but only when it benefits us.

Serving others takes the focus off of us and that could become a problem for most who are self-absorbed. We are so into ourselves that we rarely or hardly ever think about anyone but ourselves. Before you've eaten a meal, have you in the middle of grace, thanked God for the chef or the cook? The person that prepared your drink, your salad or even greeted you at the door of a restaurant? Hardly, could be most of our answer, because as I'm writing this I can't say that I have either, and even though we are being served we still have a service to render. It takes so much effort for cooks to prepare food for others, it isn't just as simple as one may think. Time and energy is a major factor to prepare something for someone who may not even eat it all.

A part of Jesus performing this miracle was not about the event or the fact that he could do it, but the mere reason was to serve in this capacity so that men would glorify his father! Most of the acts we are doing shouldn't be about us per say, but more about the fact that we do it so that God can be glorified. In the cooking industry most chefs and local cooks don't just do it because of money, but they do it because they love serving others.

As my mother and father cooked and grilled for many that would often pass through our home, I recall the love, passion and pride they took in preparing and desiring to make things great for the people they served. They wanted to make sure that when their guests left with hope to make them feel a little better about life, even if it was just for that moment.

So I leave you with this, if Jesus could serve to not only change the atmosphere at the reception in order to bring attention to his Father by way of the miracle, who's life will you change by serving them in a way to bring glory to the Father? Remember serving isn't about you, but about others! Make the impression while you can. "Love what you do and do what you love!"

Hot Chocolate

1 pack of hot chocolate mix

Milk

1 Tsp Cinnamon

1 Tsp Vanilla extract

1 Tsp Peppermint flavor or Candy can Whipped cream

2 to 3 Tsp of sugar

Directions

In a small pan, place 1 cup of milk, 1 Tsp of cinnamon, 1Tsp of vanilla extract, 1 candy cane or (peppermint flavor), stir until candy melts, *(do not allow to boil)*.

If you desire more peppermint flavor add more candy cane or more PF

Place hot chocolate mix into a mug with 2 to 3 Tsp of sugar, and add milk mixture to cup. Stir and add whip cream. Serve hot.

Ulrica's Tasty Punch

1 16oz can of 100 % Pineapple Juice

1 pack of Tropical Punch Kool-Aid

2 to 3 Cups of Sugar

1 2 Liter Ginger Ale

1 20oz of Pineapple Slices

Directions

In a punch bowl, place Kool-Aid pack and 2 to 3 cups of sugar first. Next pour 1/2 of 2 L ginger ale and the 1/2 of pineapple juice *(make sure to shake the pineapple juice first)*. Stir the mixture together and then add more of each ingredient as needed. Once the punch is complete, place pineapple slices to the punch.

J. Stearns Spritzer

1 pack of fresh black berries

Fresh mint

Ginger ale

Strawberries

100% Watermelon Juicy Juice Drink

Directions

In the bottom of a glass, place 2-3 fresh mint leaves. Add 3-4 blackberries and 1 strawberry sliced.

Fill the glass about half way full after which, fill the remaining with Juicy Juice. Top the glass with a fresh strawberry.

Note

Make sure your liquid ingredients are cold.

"Having a sweet tooth for the wrong words is dangerous to your health! Choose to speak well of others. Life is sweeter that way!"
-Jermaine L. Stearns

Sweet Words

Words of affirmation and words of encouragement can go a long way for a person whether they are in a state of happiness or a state of being down. The scriptures teach us that our words have power. In fact, it tells is that we have the ability to speak life or death. Have you ever said something to someone or have had something said to you that caused either one of you to never be the same, or maybe you have said something that just broke you and their spirit? What about having something said that caused you or a person to smile or totally feel better? Our words have the ability to change the mood or even the atmosphere. In this life there are going to be people that will desire to destroy you with their words and then there are individuals who desire for you to live properly by the choice of words.

In 2008 I had the privilege of meeting a woman who I never thought would be an aid in changing the course of my life. I was asked to attend an award ceremony for community leaders in Columbia, South Carolina and serve as one of the photographers for this event. I was honored to even be considered due to not feeling my experience as a photographer was the most polished. Never the less, I was amongst some of the who's who in my city. As we progressed in the dinner that evening, the guest speaker who was asked to encourage the community was none other than, award winner, Dori Sanders, author of the book, Clover. As a student in middle school, reading this book was a part of our curriculum and I never would have thought in a million years that I would be in the same room with the community leaders, let alone an author whose book I enjoyed! The night was coming to an end and she was available to sign and take pictures with guests. Guess what, I got an autographed copy of my childhood book and an amazing picture with the scribe. Unbeknownst to me, she had written a second book, and to seize this moment I wanted a copy as well. When I inquired of the book she informed me that she ran out of copies and asked if I didn't mind following her and her assistant back to the hotel to get one, so I did! As we entered in to the lobby we took a seat while her assistant went to retrieve the book, Ms. Sanders began to pour into me. She asked more about my personal life, like marriage, children, careers and endeavors and after that she looked me in the eye and said, when are you going to tell your story? "You have a story to tell".

Those six words left a mark on me that has brought me to a pivotal point in my life, where I am now, 10 years later telling one of my stories. You see, I walked away from that moment not realizing that a seed was planted and would spring forth and one day bear much fruit. Ms. Sanders may have no clue what she did that rainy night, or maybe she did, one thing is for sure, her words, in fact, her sweet words changed my life! My, who would think words have power?

"Encourage yourself until you convince yourself!"
-Jermaine L. Stearns

World Renown Author, Dori Sanders and Jermaine.
Photographer, Darryl Lovett

Sweet Potato Pie

4 to 5 medium sweet potatoes

1 stick butter, softened

1 1/2 cup of brown sugar

2 eggs, beaten

1 Tbsp. pure vanilla extract

1 Tbsp. ground cinnamon

1 Tbsp. ground nutmeg

3/4 cup evaporated milk

1 to 2 unbaked pie crust

Directions

Preheat oven to 350 degree F.

Boil sweet potatoes on top of stove until softened. When done, let cool. Scrape the pulp out of the skin, transfer to a large bowl, and mash. Set aside.

While still hot or warm, add butter, brown sugar, vanilla, cinnamon, nutmeg, evaporated milk until creamy, lastly add eggs and stir into sweet potatoes. Beat together with mixer until smooth or for smoother consistency put mixture into a blender and blend into a smooth consistency. Pour into an unbaked pie shell.

Bake on bottom rack of oven for 1 hour or until center of pie is firm. Serve warm!

Life Nugget

The word nugget can be defined as a small lump of gold or other precious metal found ready-formed in the earth. McDonald's, one of the leading fast food restaurants in the business, developed a similar concept of little golden items in a box, these are known as chicken nuggets. Have you ever had a craving for something small but it gave you big satisfaction?

There have been many big, yet little, things that seemed so small but they served such a huge purpose in life. We have come to know them as life nuggets! My mother used to say things like, "that red thing in your mouth is going to get you in trouble one day!" "I'm not a toy, don't play with me!" and things like, "Do it now, so you won't have to do it later." Simple, yet satisfying! The Bible is full of these life nuggets. "Don't cast your pearls before swine!" "Be not conformed to this world, but be ye transformed by the renewing your mind!" The principle of life nuggets is to just give you a little to get you through. You see, a four piece nugget box may not be a full course meal, but is compacted with just enough to get you through. Life can often bring challenges, many ups and downs, and highs and lows that can really convince you to not refresh yourself to get through. This is when you have to dig into your little box of nuggets. While at the time of being given nuggets you may think, this isn't going to fill me up, nor is this going to have value or be enough substance. But just at the right time, those little nuggets make a huge difference.

It's not at the moments of being strong that the nuggets mean anything, but it is at the weakest moments when what you think will not fill you up, makes you feel so full and content. The Bible and words of wisdom for the wise are filled with those golden precious metals that are small but hold so much value. Take a moment to reflect on the last nugget you consumed at your darkest, most vulnerable, emptiest moment, and how it gave you so much joy! Tasted good right? It's not the size of the nugget that matters, it's the value that matters.

You may not think your life matters or that where you are right now counts. I encourage you to dig into your little box of nuggets or even take a moment and develop your own ability to feed yourself, but don't be stingy, make sure you share with others. You never know, your little box could be the turn around to bring much profit to you and to a nation.

Bible Reference: Mark 7:6

Grilled Fruit

Fresh Pineapple

Fresh Mango

Directions

Slice and peel fruit and place on hot grill, 2 to 4 minutes on each side. Serve Warm!

Helpful Tip

The fruit's natural sugars will come forth! A little brown sugar never hurt, however taste and see, for the natural sweetness may outweigh the addition.

Stuffed Chocolate Croissants

1 can of refrigerated croissants

1 8 pack of Hershey's mini chocolate bars Butter

Cinnamon

Powdered sugar

Directions

Unroll the can of croissants separating them into 8 flat pieces. Place a bar of chocolate into the center of each one and roll to cover the chocolate. Once covered, sprinkle cinnamon to taste on top of each croissant. Place them into a greased dish with butter and cook according to the package or until golden brown on top.

Once completed, top each one with hot butter and then sprinkle powdered sugar on top to taste.

Serve warm!

Yogurt Parfait

Shortbread Cookies

Strawberry yogurt

Peach yogurt

Fresh strawberries

Fresh blueberries Kiwi

Whipped cream

Directions

Cut all fruit to your desirable size. Layer the cup as follows:
Shortbread cookies

Yogurt

Mixed fruit

Keep layering until you reach the top, Upon reaching the top, sprinkle some shortbread cookie crumbles on top and whipped cream. Serve.

Service With A Smile

Several occasions I can recall my mom and Aunt Carolyn Jean making plans to sell dinners. They called it selling dinners, I called it hustling, now that's what it was, an honest living! They had their game plan set, they got the list together on what they were going to sell and how much they needed along with how much these dinners were going to cost.

Now before we could go any further, you must understand the character of my mom and auntie together! They went together like salt and pepper, hash and rice, corn and butter, and at times they didn't mix at all, just like oil and water. But you couldn't dare talk about them. My mom was next to the baby out of eight siblings and Aunt Carolyn I believe was the 3rd oldest girl! She was a thin lady with short reddish blonde hair (most of the time) with a lot of spunk about herself. Not only could she cook, but she could play some spades, dance and and boy she was the life of the party. Aunt Carolyn was so full of life and she was our Aunt! For us as her nephews, I believe most of our favorite dish from her was her macaroni and cheese! Now my mom could throw down on a mac and cheese too, but I secretly liked Aunt Carolyn's better! Combining all that laughter and fun in the kitchen was a sight to see, let alone the taste of the food!

I'm not quite sure whose idea it was to sell the dinners but whoever's it was, they made it work! I could recall the fried or baked chicken dinner sales. You had chicken of your choice and side of green beans, potato salad, roll and a slice of store bought cake. Oh, and don't forget to add a soda for $.50. Now my dad would do the frying if he was off, Auntie would be on potato salad, and mom would do the beans and baked chicken...TEAMWORK!

They would sell on Thursdays and Fridays. The purpose behind this was that it was in line with the garbage service payday. My aunt and uncle owned a garbage service that was passed down from my grandfather and after he passed my aunt and uncle inherited it. It later passed to my cousins. Since their pay period was on a Thursday, my mom and aunt figured they could maximize their opportunity of sales if they sold to the sanitation crew on their lunch and pay period. It was a master plan! They would have my cousin take orders and I would deliver. They even had ME on delivery!

The kitchen would be jumping, music playing, aroma in the air and a beer or two on the table. Making it happen! Operation hours were from 11ish to about 4ish, nonstop! The phone would be ringing and their pockets would be singing. I never knew how much they would make but it was enough for them to keep the tradition going. My mom and aunt got along well, and I have often heard them fuss a little but not too much when it came down to those dinner sales. They were about business, it was like a real restaurant without hairnets and gloves. It was something I will always remember.

As their business began to spread, so did the menu and even the locations. We went from the garbage service, to barbershops and daycares, up and down Farrow Road. They went from selling chicken and beans to spaghetti dinners, and on one occasion, fried fish dinners. If they didn't have anything in common they had cooking. The money was good but I enjoyed the way they laughed and loved on each other in the process. They were some of the best cooks in the family, so I guess this is where I get some of my cooking styles from.

My Aunt and mom would give you the shirt of their backs and do almost anything for you; just good hearted Wilson Girls. My aunt loved her nieces and nephews and we all can literally say we have a story with Aunt Carolyn Jean! I can recall when I wanted to pledge and needed the money. It was my mom and auntie who sold dinners for me to get half of the money. Another time when I was going to Africa to study abroad, they went at it again, making over five hundred dollars' worth of spending money for Africa. Of course, Auntie got her cut, but rightfully so. She wanted me to go just as bad as I did. Not many people will be your pusher, or stand in your corner to support you, but watching these two in the kitchen helped me to become a better man. Even though they are both gone now, their lessons and instructions of a little dash of this and a sprinkle of that, and teaspoons of help still linger on. Their inspiration and motivation haven't gone unnoticed. I honor theme for being my personal chefs.

Aunt Carolyn Jean chilling after cooking.

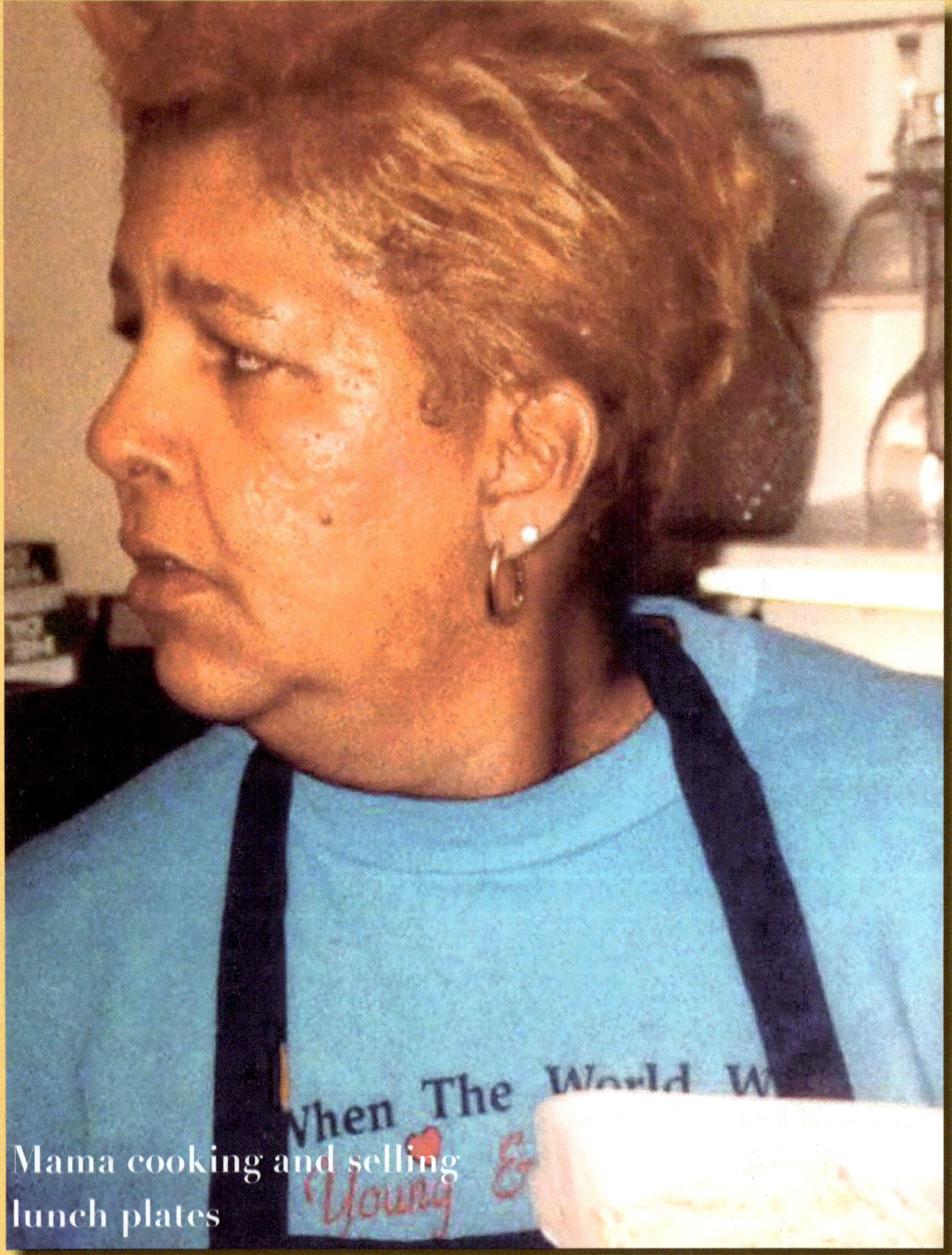

Mama cooking and selling lunch plates

"YOU HAVE A STORY TO TELL! TELL YOUR STORY!"
-Dori Sanders

Take Time

Singing on the porch, music in the background, or cards being shuffled, and occasionally drinks on the table was a part of my world. Arguments to make ups, death to births, all occurred in my family, as it does in almost every family! As I reflect on some of these, the question I'm left with often is how did we make it through all that?

I come from a large family. My mother was one of eight and when I was born I became one of three children and one of 22 grandchildren. On my father's side, he was one of five, and I become the eldest of 13 grandchildren. So you can gather being a part of family was my life. Man, we were really close growing up. We would spend the night over at each other's houses, go to the pool together, you name it, we probably did it. And then life happened! Individuals got married, had children, and moved forward, so people now start to step into their own and even though they are distant they're never too far away from family.

Most of the time in families, the most common time to reconnect with family members is when a loved one passed away and a family reunion occurs, not because of planning and scheduling, but due to unfortunate events, and you wonder to yourself, why do we only have to come together in times like these? You see, the value of family only exists as long as the family members push to keep it together. Having been married for 10 years, I've come to realize that at the end of the day, unity and love makes up a family even if they are not blood-related.

On this journey I have been blessed with so many different sets of families. There are the ones I was born into, The Wilson & The Stearns, and then God connected me with spiritual families, such as The Butler Family(Clinton, NC), The FSU Family(Gospel & Concert Choir), The Floyd Family(Ma Ruby, Tara, Charlese), The Alexander Family, & The Hope Family, The Brother & Sisters Family(Kelly's, Brantley's, Benton's, Berry's, Burnette's, McLaughlin/Aaron) & The VCDC Family. You see, God has a way of allowing family to derive from a diverse group of people. Even though all of my families don't know each other, they are all God-centered and God-ordained.

The truth of the matter is that we need someone. Not all families are good families, we must be honest with ourselves. Some families we are born into and have no choice about being a part of it, and then there are the extended ones that become family but not by blood.

When God sent Roni Stearns in my life I never knew the joy of becoming a man and experiencing love with my life partner. She has been a true example of love and compassion and so much so she gave birth to my beautiful children. They have shaped my world, and even sometimes I may not understand either of them, they are my family! They have shown me what unity and love is all about!

I encourage you today to take a moment to reflect on who's in your family and what they mean to you, even if they are not blood related. If they have some value in your life, take time and spend with them. Laugh, smile, cry, disagree with respect, love unconditionally with them, for life is o short to be trying to love on someone who is no longer with you. Remember you only get one family! Treasure the tree, while the roots are producing life.

Lonnell's Tomato Pie

1 to 2 Pie crusts

2 red or yellow frim tomatoes

1 cup of mayo

1 cup shredded cheese (cheddar or 3 cheeses)

Salt

Pepper

Directions

Preheat oven to 350 degrees.

Slice and season tomatoes, and place in pie crust. In a separate bowl, mix mayo and cheese together, once mixed, cover tomatoes and place in oven.

Allow to bake for 25-30 minutes, or until cheese and crust are golden brown.

Serve Warm!

Seared Steak

"Be cautious of those who associate with your enemies, for they could be one step away from becoming your enemy as well!"
-Jermaine L. Stearns

Seared Steak

Steak of Choice (Ribeye)
1 Fuji apple
1 onion
Red bell pepper
Salt Pepper Basil
Rosemary

Directions

Season steak with seasoning ingredients to desired taste on both sides. In skillet, place 1tsp of EVOO, and place steak into pan, searing on both sides for about 2 to 4 minutes or until nicely seared.

Once seared, add 2 TBS of butter to steak and place chopped red peppers, onions and sliced apple into pan. Cover and allow to cook for another 3 minutes on medium heat.

Then take the cover off and place into oven, still in pan until steak is cooked to your desire. Remove from oven and allow steak to sit for a moment to allow the juices to set in.

Serve with a side of your choice. I recommend, fresh greens or cabbage and skillet potatoes.

Turkey Wings

2.5 lbs turkey wings, cut into sections if whole

2 Tbsp olive oil

1 Tbsp onion powder

2 tsp seasoning salt

1 1/2 Tbsp paprika

2 tsp parsley flakes

2 tsp poultry seasoning

2 Tbsp Salt

2 Tbsp Pepper

1 onion diced

Directions

Season wings with all seasonings, and place in a roasting bag. Cook in oven for 45 minutes. Once wings are done, remove from roasting bag and place back in dish and turn oven on broil. Broil for about 5-10 minutes.

Serve hot!

Cornish Hens

Two Cornish hens

Roasting bag

Potatoes

Sweet onion

Carrots

Celery

Salt Pepper

2 lemons

Directions

Pre-heat oven 350 Degrees. Season hens with salt, pepper, paltry seasoning, inside and out (as desired).

Cut lemons in half and stuff inside hens along with vegetables.

Place in roasting bag and cook in oven for about 45 minutes.

This meal goes great with rice pilaf and a big slice of cornbread!

Daddy Daddie's Meatloaf

Oil, for greasing dish

1 (10-ounce) box chopped spinach, thawed and drained

1 onion, diced

2 1/2 pounds ground turkey

2 eggs

1/3 cup Worcestershire sauce

2 Tbsp. chopped parsley leaves

1 tsp salt

1 tsp cracked black pepper

1 (8-ounce) can tomato sauce

1/2 cup shredded cheese (cheddar)

1/4 cup of brown sugar

1/2 cup of breadcrumbs

Directions

In a large bowl, combine the onion, turkey, eggs, Worcestershire, parsley, salt, and pepper. Mix until well combined.

Transfer half of the mixture to the casserole dish and shape it into a medium-sized log. Using your fingers, make an indentation in the meat for the filling. This should resemble a canoe. In the indentation place the shredded cheese, then add the remaining meat to cover. Form the meatloaf, being sure to cover the filling completely with meat. Pour the tomato sauce over the meatloaf, then top with brown sugar.

Bake in the oven for about 55 to 60 minutes. Remove the meatloaf from the oven and let it sit for 10 minutes before slicing and serving.

Mickey's & Regina's Oven Cabbage

1 head of Cabbage

EVOO or butter

Salt

Pepper

Garlic Powder

1/2 Basil

1 onion

Directions

Oven preheated 350 degrees

Slice your cabbage and place in a bowl. Drizzle with EVOO, season with salt, pepper, garlic powder, and basil. Toss around with hands!

Taste to make sure it's seasoned to your liking! Remember eating raw cabbage will not hurt you

Place on cooking sheet, bake in the oven for about 25 minutes, turning often. Cook until its nice and tender.

Stove Top

Large Frying Pan, coat bottom of pan with butter and EVOO, placed chopped cabbage and onion into hot pan and season to taste, cover pan and cook on medium heat until tender.

Grilled Fish

Fish of choice

Salt

Pepper

Fresh garlic

Parsley

Directions

Fresh or thawed fish, placed in its own individual aluminum foil packet (See Veggie Pack). Season all fish to taste and place 1/2 Tbsp of butter in each packet. Seal tightly and place on grill until fish is thoroughly cooked and tender.

Serve in open packet

Grilled Shrimp

8-19 lb Shrimp

Melted butter mix

1 cup of butter

1/2 tsp Garlic

1/2 tsp Old Bay seasoning

1 Tbsp. parsley

Butter Mixture

Melt butter and add your garlic, Old Bay and parsley to butter, stir and taste. Add more if desired.

Directions

Place thawed shrimp on kabobs sticks, (up to 5 to 6 shrimp, per kabob). Place on hot grill and turn within 2 minutes. Once turn, base the shrimp with melted butter, garlic, and Old Bay seasoning.

"Your emotions can cost you the kingdom!"
-Jermaine L. Stearns

Which Way Should I Go?

Have you ever thought about what you would eat, way in advance, and in your mind you start thinking off all the wonderful foods that you enjoy? It gets so good to you that you even traveled the distance to make this craving become a reality?

Often times in life we wonder what life will bring us next; next career, next relationship, next financial breakthrough. The word declares that we should take no thought of tomorrow for tomorrow will take care of itself. God exemplifies his provision by informing us that he is our tomorrow and our source! He is the provider that sustains us in every area of our lives. It's simply because of who he is, that represents his provision.

God even goes further and tells us that if he can provide for the lilies of the fields and the fowl of the air, that he for sure would take care of us! You see, the difference between the fields and fowl is that we, unlike them, were created out of his image. Don't you think that if God created us to look, sound, and smell like him, that he would take care of us, which is he?

You see, it is a part of our DNA and genetic makeup to crave, but we must crave the right things. God tells his children not to worry simply because he is our tomorrow, and that he has already provided all that we would ever need. While we crave natural foods, we also need to make sure that the spiritual craving of worshipping and communion with our heavenly father is fulfilled. How do we quench this craving? We must do whatever it takes to make sure we feed that spiritual craving! Read our word daily, keep an open line of communication with God (through prayer), open our heart to him in the secret chambers, and worship him for who he is!

Yes, this food is good, but there is nothing that can compare to the spiritual growth that will satisfy your soul. As you mediate on the tastes of these foods, reflect on how much more your spiritual belly will be satisfied.

Chicken Broccoli Alfredo

4 to 5 chicken breast
Fresh Broccoli
Sundried Tomatoes
5 Slices of Bacon
1 16oz box of bowtie or fettucine pasta
1 Tbsp of Parsley

Salt, Pepper, Basil

Alfredo Sauce

1 16oz Heavy Cream
1/2 tsp black pepper
1 tsp onion powder,
1 tsp garlic
1 cup of melted butter
1 1/2 cup of Italian shredded cheese

Directions

Pasta
Add pasta of choice to salted, boiling water until pasta is tender (do not over cook pasta). Drain pasta but keep hot water from pasta and blanch the broccoli in the water until tender.

*Do not overcook broccoli for you may cook away the nutrients

Bacon & Chicken
In a pan, cook bacon until crispy, remove bacon and leave the grease in pan, add seasoned chicken breast to hot grease and cook chicken breast until cooked all the way through.

Once cooked throughout allow chicken to rest before cutting. Once rested cut into cubes.

Alfredo Sauce

In separate pot, add 1 cup of melted butter, heavy cream, and season with pepper, onion powered, and garlic. Allow to heat and once heated, remove from stove and add your shredded cheese and stir.

Once mixed well, marry the alfredo sauce, pasta together, chicken cubes, and broccoli. Plate these items and add bacon and sundried tomatoes on top and serve with a slice of French grilled bread.

"When we recognize our weakness that's when we actually become our strongest!"
-Jermaine L. Stearns

Twisted Spaghetti

EVOO (Extra Virgin Olive Oil)
1 lb. (8oz) Spaghetti Sauce
1 lb. Thin spaghetti noodles
3/4 cup of portabella mushroom (roughly chopped)
3/4 cup of onions (chopped)
1/4 cup green onions
1 green bell pepper(chopped)
1 to 3 Italian sausage links
1lb lean ground turkey
1/2 tsp of oregano
Salt & Pepper
1 tsp fresh garlic
2 Tbsp. sugar

Directions

In a large pan on medium, add the 1 to 2 Tbsp. of EVOO and place the 1-3 Italian sausage link to pan. Let sausage cook until all the way done. (Suggestions: you may want to cover them will cooking, so the steam can assist with the cooking process).

Once the sausage links are done, remove them and allow them to sit. In the same pan add the onions, peppers, mushrooms. (Note: you may need to add a little more EVOO to the pan to keep vegetables from sticking.) Season the vegetables as they cook with salt and pepper (to taste), Place the 1/2 tsp of oregano and the 1tsp of garlic to mix.

After vegetables have cooked until tender, remove from the pan and add the ground turkey. Cook the turkey until completely brown. **(You may desire to add more salt to taste)**, When the ground turkey is completely cooked, add your salted vegetables to the turkey, then add your spaghetti sauce. Allow to simmer for 3 minutes.

Cut the sausage links into coins and place them into the mix. Allow to simmer for another 3 minutes and then add the sugar(Note: add to taste if necessary).

Add 4-5 cups of water into a pot. Add a 1 Tbsp. of EVOO and 1 Tbsp of Butter to water, and bring to a boil. Once boiling add 2 tsp of salt and the add the noodles. Cook them until tender, 3-5 minutes.

Serving

Plate the noodles and add the sauce on top. Add graded cheese and for topping, 1 tsp of parsley sprinkled over the cheese.

"The heart of the call must be greater than the heart of the gift."
-Jermaine L. Stearns

Shrimp Linguine

Large raw shrimp

1 box of thin spaghetti

3 Lemons

White cooking wine

Parsley

Salt

Pepper

Butter

Cilantro

2 tsp EVOO

Directions

Season shrimp with salt, pepper, and garlic! Sautee on each side until golden brown.

Add 4-5 cups of water into a pot. Add a 1Tbsp of EVOO and 1 Tbsp. of butter to water, and bring to a boil. Once boiling add 2 Tbsp. of salt and then add the noodles. Cook them until tender, 3-5 minutes, drain water completely.

Once complete place 1tsp of butter and cooked noodles in the pan you sautéed the shrimp in. Add shrimp, and white cooking wine to loosen noodles, 2 Tbsp. of parsley and cilantro to mixture. Upon completion squeeze 2 lemons on shrimp and noodles. Plate meal and place sliced lemon on top for garnish. This meal can be served hot or cold!

"Jesus said, we are the salt of the Earth!"-Jesus Christ, The Bible We as believers should be causing hypertension in the world!"
-Jermaine L. Stearns

Bible Reference: Matthew 5:13

Garlic Mashed Potatoes

8 Golden Potatoes

1/2 Tbsp. Salt

1/2 Tbsp. pepper

1/2 Tbsp. of garlic

1/2 cup of milk

3/4 butter

1 Tbsp. of parsley

Directions

Peel your potatoes and cut them into quarters, adding to boiling water. Once potatoes are cooked fully, drain the water off the potatoes and return them back to the pot.

Mash potatoes while still hot, leaving little chunks in the mix. After which, add butter, salt and pepper. Stir and taste! After tasting, add your milk and parsley. Once completed, then serve hot!

"Don't give up in the process of overcoming!"
-Jermaine L. Stearns

Grilled Chicken Breast

Fresh Chicken Breast
Salt
Pepper
Paprika
Basil
1 to 3 oranges

Directions
Season chicken with ingredients, on both sides (allow to marinate in refrigerator overnight for best flavor).

You can cook these several ways. Two of the best ways are to either grill them or sear them in a lightly greased pan. Once they have been cooked all the way through, squeeze fresh orange juice on them.

Remember once chicken is cooked to perfection allow them to sit for about 3 minutes and serve.

Grilled Chicken Wings

8 to 10 Chicken Wings
1 Tbsp. salt
1 1/2 Tbsp. Pepper
1 Tbsp. Paprika
1/2 cup of Worcestershire sauce
1/2 tsp Rosemary
1/2 cup of Brown Sugar
1/4 cup of EVOO

Directions

Take your chicken wings, place them into a zip lock bag, and pour all of your ingredients into the bag. Place into refrigerator up to 4 hours or allow to sit over night for better results.

Prepare your grill and allow coals to turn almost white! This means the coals are good and hot and are ready for the chicken. Cook and serve with a smile!

Carolyn's Mac & Cheese

1 or 1/2 box of elbow macaroni shells

1 stick of butter

1 can of condensed milk

Salt

Pepper

3 cups of shredded cheese

2 eggs

Directions

Preheat the oven to 350 degrees F.

Cook the macaroni until still slightly firm. Drain and while warm, add stick of butter, condensed milk and season with salt and pepper to taste, Add 2 cups of cheese to noodles and 2 eggs. Mix together.

Transfer to greased dish and top with 1 cup of cheese. And season with black pepper. Bake for 20-25 minutes until browned and bubbly.

Until Forever

My Dearest...

Wow, can you believe I am about to become a published author? I got a few finished but this one will be the first published. I'm so excited about all that God has allowed me to experience in these last seven months. I had to bring up the thoughts of smells, laughter and final goodbyes, but it was all worth it to get to this point. My final thoughts and prayers on January 26th, 2007 was, God please allow her blood pressure to come back to normal, God please allow here breathing to slow, God please allow the pressure to be released off her body and give her peace. Who would have thought after a faint noise over the respirator you would expire? You, see we didn't get to talk that day, but I knew you were listening, and your mere unspoken words spoke loudly!

I know we hadn't spoken in a while, and that's not my fault, well it's nobody's fault, but nevertheless, here we are. To get you caught up on things, I finally stepped into my calling of becoming a preacher, you remember when you asked me when I was going to preach? Well, it happen Ma! Not only am I licensed, but I'm an ordained elder who is now pastoring. Oh, I got married!!! Yep, I did, to that young girl I told you about when I came home from school and you told me to wait awhile. I never knew why, but I'm glad I did wait! I knew you couldn't make it but we had a special place for you at the ceremony, and out of that union, you have three beautiful grandchildren.

One of them has your name as their middle name, Jerni Lonnell, how about that?

So much has happened in the last ten years, yea I know it's been that long, but I never stop thinking about you! Ma, I got my degree!!! I finally finished, I know you were there with me at Fayetteville State University unpacking my bags and stuff, but I didn't finish there. Life happened and I believe God had other plans. But I got it! I am a graduate of Andersonville Theological Seminary.
Ma, I believe you would be so proud. I knew you couldn't come but I had a special place for you right on the same row I was sitting on. Man, how I miss you! Dad is doing well, he has gotten married again to a beautiful woman, and Ma I believe you would love her! She keeps him in line and takes no prisoners, she is just great!! Monica is her name, in fact I married them, so you know it had to be the right person (smiling). Just about everyone was there. Daddy is in a difference space, and it's good.

My brothers are doing the best they can, but I have some not so good news for you, Pooh is no longer with us! He passed away October 2016. It was all unexpected, crushed us all, and I we are still trying to recover. MJ, Nicole and Madison are doing the best they can, you know I know this all too well. I will say this though Ma, his funeral brought us all back together, all your kids and grandchildren. Death has a way right? Kenny is well, I speak with and see him every now and again. He has his life, but we do speak often on Facebook. Oh, that's a new site that has everyone captivated lol. We are all we have so, we make it work.

Life for me has been pretty well, I had you for a mother and Dad is a great father. I have spiritual friends and family that make sure we are taken care of, oh and I got the Holy Ghost, so I'm alright lol. I plan on writing more books, creating more t-shirts (JLive, 'Jesus Live') and keep taking pictures, something you would press me to do, you remember? I want to go back to school to the highest level I can and when I retire and your grandchildren are off to college, your daughter-n-law and I will be millionaires by that time so we are going to travel and enjoy Jesus, hallelu-.

Well Ma, I've got to go now, it's late here and the kids will be up before you know it. But before I go, thank you for teaching me how to cook, clean and even on your sick bed, allowing me to take care of you. God said there was a purpose, didn't understand it then, but I got it now. Thank you for you being you and loving me unconditionally even with my deepest secrets. Love you to the moon! Remember to take care of yourself, until forever... and in your favorite words, "I'm on a mission and I'm going fishing!"

Your son!

About the Author

Jermaine Stearns is the proud son of Mr. Benjamin Stearns and the late Lonnell Stearns. Raised in Columbia South Carolina, he is the youngest sibling of three boys. Elder Stearns attended Fayetteville State University, where he majored in General Music with a Vocal Concentration and minored in Biology. He has received a Bachelor of Ministry from Andersonville Theology Seminary.

Elder Stearns accepted his calling in 2005 and in December 2007, he was licensed at Morris Creek Baptist Church under Dr. William Abell, where he served as one of the Youth Ministers and Minister of Music.

In July 2009, Elder Stearns founded C.O.L.O.R C.O.D.E Youth Ministry of Hope Christian Church, Fayetteville NC, where his pastor was Elder Sandra D. Kirkman.

On October 27th 2013, Elder Jermaine Stearns was ordained as an Elder under Hope Fellowship International, and leadership of Dr. Wayman J. Kirkman Sr, Presiding Bishop.

Pastor Stearns and his wife are the founding leaders of Victorious Christian Deliverance Center, known as V.C.D.C Ministries, currently located in Hope Mills, North Carolina.

His goals and aspirations are to continue to help make a difference in the lives of young men and to carry out God's word. Elder Stearns Is the Owner and Chief Photographer of The JL3 Brand, in Fayetteville, NC. His work has been featured in local advertisements, billboards, magazines, websites, and CD and book covers. He is the founder of the I Am Beautiful Campaign for young girls and the Tiger Paw Mentoring Academy for young boys at Sunnyside Elementary School.

He is happily married to Minister Roni D. Stearns and is the proud father of Jerni Lonnell, Jordan Lily Stearns, and Josiah Levi Stearns.

www.ingramcontent.com/pod-product-compliance
Lightning Source LLC
Chambersburg PA
CBHW061814290426
44110CB00026B/2870